# Can I Pet Your Dog?

by jeremy nguyen

CHRONICLE BOOKS
SAN FRANCISCO

Library of Congress Cataloging-in-Publication Data
Names: Nguyen, Jeremy, author, illustrator.
Title: Can I pet your dog? / by Jeremy Nguyen.
Description: San Francisco : Chronicle Books, [2022]
Identifiers: LCCN 2022013254 | ISBN 9781797217536 (hardcover)
Subjects: LCSH: Dogs. | Dogs--Pictorial works.
Classification: LCC SF427 .N49 2022 | DDC 636.7--dc23/eng/20220413
LC record available at https://lccn.loc.gov/2022013254ISBN 978-1-7972-1753-6

Manufactured in China.

Design by Maggie Edelman.

10 9 8 7 6 5 4 3 2

Chronicle Books LLC
680 Second Street
San Francisco, CA 94107
www.chroniclebooks.com

Dedicated to Lava, Natasha, and everyone who let me pet their dog

# Introduction

Taking a walk for twenty minutes a day is a well-known exercise that every doctor would prescribe for its health benefits. You can leave the house and get outside, enjoy the fresh air, and get that heart rate up. One health benefit doctors fail to mention is that you might even get to pet someone else's dog, which is by far the most effective medicine of all time.

You may not have a dog or even know someone with a dog, but step foot outside and you're bound to come across a good boy or girl eventually. And when that eventuality occurs, you may feel a sudden overwhelming *need to pet that dog*, and you'll do anything to make it happen. You might try to entice the dog at the next table with some of your leftovers. You may loiter in dog parks with no dog of your own, just to get some pats in. Maybe you'll even scale a building or walk across hot coals to get a piece of that dog. To each their own. The point is, most of us will do anything to pet someone else's dog. If you've exhausted all the usual earthly methods, what follows may inspire you; but be careful—there are some unhinged, dangerous, and scientifically advanced techniques that should not be attempted unless you are a certified and licensed card-carrying, dog-petting professional.

All jokes aside, you should always ask the dog's human if it's okay first, then let the dog judge you with some sniffs before you proceed with friendly petting. Before approaching a dog in public, it is important to know if that dog is working and should not be distracted. Service dogs, for example, perform specific tasks or services for humans with disabilities. In other cases, a working dog may be a therapy dog, whose entire job is to provide comfort and affection to those who need it. A therapy dog may be found in nursing homes, hospitals, disaster-relief areas, shelters, and other places where their hard work is needed. If you are not sure if a dog is working or not, you should always ask!

Ask nicely.

Make noise.

Food always works.

Make noise, but squeakier.

Scope out the most interesting party guests.

Apologize for your lack of grace.

Make noise, but—you get the point.

Always offer to dogsit.

Send your friends away, if you have to.

Lie.

Use your hot friends as a distraction.

Be sure to keep good relations with your neighbors.

Find the best angles.

Ask nicely.

Make home improvements.

Play for the audience you want.

Take a holistic approach.

Be more relatable.

Be more enticing.

Be more daring.

Seek help.

Get into landscaping.

Don't be afraid to do some dirty work.

Try your hand at robotics.

It's important to stay discreet.

Blend in with your surroundings.

Take initiative.

Whoops, that's a cat.

Embrace herd mentality.

BYOH (Bring Your Own Hoops)

Get fast and furr-ious.

Advertise.

Be resourceful.

Creativity is key.

Track and field:
Track down a dog;
field traffic.

No land? No problem. Take to the sea!

Or the sky!

Try your hand at perfumery.

Bone up on history.

Take advantage of technological advancements.

Rub shoulders with the high rollers.

Don't forget to keep in touch with your friends.

Let the algorithm take over.

## About the Author

Jeremy Nguyen is a cartoonist and illustrator living in Brooklyn, NY. He has been contributing cartoons and drawings to *The New Yorker* magazine since 2017, and his work has appeared on *The Nib*, *Wired*, and *The Guardian*. He has illustrated several books for Penguin Random House, ABRAMS Books, and Callisto Books, as well as board games for AEG Games and WizKids! Jeremy currently does not have a dog but wants one, and in the meantime, he likes to pet many neighborhood dogs. His best friend is a dog named Lava.